T0208534

UNRAVEL

UNRAVƎL

The Misconceptions
Of Dating Into Marriage According To The Word God

"A practical Dating Guide for Christian Men and Women"

STACEY TOUCHSTONE

UNRAVEL
THE MISCONCEPTIONS OF DATING INTO MARRIAGE
ACCORDING TO THE WORD GOD "A PRACTICAL DATING
GUIDE FOR CHRISTIAN MEN AND WOMEN"

Scripture quotations from the Holy Bible, King James Version (Authorized Version). First published in 1611. Quoted from the KJV Classic Reference Bible.

iUniverse books may be ordered through booksellers or by contacting:

iUniverse
1663 Liberty Drive
Bloomington, IN 47403
www.iuniverse.com
1-800-Authors (1-800-288-4677)

ISBN: 978-1-5320-9121-6 (sc)
ISBN: 978-1-5320-9122-3 (e)

Library of Congress Control Number: 2020910028

Print information available on the last page.

iUniverse rev. date: 06/11/2020

Thank you to my wonderful daughter Brianna for always believing her Mama can do anything!

To my family and friends for your belief, love and support!

Finally, it's on paper! Since writing this book I've grown spiritually in ways I never knew I would, and you will too!

This book is to educate Christian singles all over this universe who would like to date the right way, according to the word of God. Learn the order of the dating groundwork that it takes to develop a relationship that has a designed purpose… Marriage. In order to live in a Spirit led marriage, it is vital to have this knowledge **before** you take the vows. By doing so it will help to considerably lower divorce rates, and produce marriages that will produce children that have seen their parents believe and live this kind of life; now they believe and live the same type of life and on to the next generation and the next generation until Jesus comes!

Welcome to
"Unravel…the misconceptions of dating into
Marriage-according to the word of God."

This journey of wanting to give love and be loved has been challenging. I've always thought that giving love would help cure EVERYTHING! Well it will, but now I understand after twenty-three years of not receiving love from the men I was involved with, that it had nothing to do with receiving love from them, but everything to do with accepting myself and God's love for me. In order to give, you must know how to receive because you can't give what you don't have...although we try!! Also, I knew I should and could have more of not just love, but of everything. I had to find out why I wanted more. How was I going to get more and what am I going to do with it when I get it? So, I was thinking it out... I needed more money... that would afford me more choices, being spiritually and biblically sound would keep me in peace. Being physically fit would allow me to really enjoy success when I finally achieved it, and I definitely needed a lot of **Love**, which motivates all parts of me! I wanted to find out how to have and balance it all. For me, giving love has always been my highest priority. I found myself compromising and taking ALL, trying to receive love... giving my "pearls" to the swine, my "honey" to the bees, and my "cookie" to the cookie monsters.....lol! My focus was so lopsided because I thought I knew what love was. I thought, because I "felt" love for him I was suppose to show him by making him feel good with sex, being nice, sharing everything I had.... yes!, and I thought I was suppose to get the same in return, right? Well, it never <u>really</u> turned out that way. So I had to learn how to say no and not feel guilty about it, and I had to stop caring about hurting his feelings. The truth is...his feelings weren't hurt, because his selfishness came before his feelings. And it turns out – "at the end of the day" what I wanted, thought and needed was not his main concern...his wife was! Or in another case, he had to decide who would be the priority for that week or month, so he could get what he needed at that time! Now I know there are some women reading this and saying, "Oh no!" I have never been in that position nor would I ever allow those things to happen to me. Yep! Some of you are saying, "How does she look?" Contrary to what you have been taught, told or heard, being treated good or bad, doesn't happen because of a look; it happens because of what you choose to <u>accept…being treated good or bad.</u> I've been a hair stylist over twenty years and I've shared some of my relationship stories with my clients and they have shared some with me. The saying "only my hairstylist knows," goes far beyond hair secrets! One of my clients, a beautiful lady, shared with me that she was dating her man for two years; bragging about how great their relationship was, only to realize she was not the only one, but the third one! A friend of mine found out after being married for five years she wasn't married, because he never got divorced from his first wife! Oh, and the most popular story I've heard… she's living with the father of her two kids, thinking she's getting married "next year" (now it's been 5 years), and she finds out the reason they haven't gotten married is because he's still messing around with his other kids' mother, who is pregnant, again! Now that makes five children… "but I just love that man", she says. All this is going on in "your" life at 40!! I could go on and on with the stories I've heard, but I have one more… *This is one of the conversations that helped to change my thinking (about the way a man thinks) and truly helped me to determine what to and what not to accept!* One day in the shop, we were listening to the radio, a talk show was on and they were talking to married men about cheating. The radio personality asked "would the other woman ever become the wife?" A listener called in and he said, "NO, she will never become the wife and get the number one position?" That's not where she started. She accepted the number two position and she knew that was what she was accepting, and if I got a divorce, she would stay in her position and I would find a new wife!" I said, **shut up**! **That shook my soul! The light came on!** I was sitting there in a daze, so many of my questions were answered, *instantly*…..and I haven't been the same since! I had no idea this was the mindset of the majority of men, married or not! Ladies, don't act like you knew that men felt like this all along! Because if you, I, "we" did - we would never consciously put ourselves in the number two position knowing that this is the bottom line! I must say, I thought I was aware but

I couldn't have been, because I would have never accepted a number two position. For me, although he never said "I'm leaving my wife so we can be together," *somehow, it felt like it would end up that way. Ladies,* "whatever you accept" from day one, that's what you will get from him for the rest of the relationship...until... Men, I'm not praising or dogging you here, but let me say; stop looking, accepting and/or preying on "number two women." Not only are you putting yourself in a compromising position, but also you have opened the door for this to happen to your daughters. Also your sons may continue in what you started. All of this pertains to all men, not only the worldly men and women, but especially the ones in church. I was one of those women in the church. That's why I can surely tell you, when you turn from all of that, and do the will of God, which is His word, change will come. I've heard the saying, when you know better you do better. Not true. Many people just know better, but you must choose to do better! I'm not going to tell you change is easy, but it is achievable!

> Your conscious is directly connected to your understanding. You will only operate in what you understand...
>
> Proverbs 3

CONTENTS

CHAPTER 1

I PROCLAIM "CHANGE!"

I Corinthians 13 KJV

My desire to understand how to fix what was wrong in my life started this change. I was operating out of order, not using my "know better," "hope'n and a pray'n" that God would fix it. So, one day I was sitting in church frustrated because I wasn't where I wanted to be in my life..I was ready to move forward, not knowing how to or even what that looked liked. Then I heard my pastor say "never stop dreaming." Then I heard him say, your decisions shouldn't be based on your feelings or someone else's; instead they must be parallel with the word of God. *"This resonated with me because I always thought that my feelings were valid enough to move on. But dealing with my feelings, in the next 15 minutes I heard or would read something that made me feel different. I'm thinking... reasoning... now I'm confused. This is why my final answer has to be based on what the word of God says about who I am and what I am to do.* Then he asked, "What problem are you here to solve? What is your purpose? What is it that you never get tired of doing? What are you passionate about?" **I remember writing, love and relationships.** I bought the DVD, went home and immediately started writing down the answers to those questions. I still watch it, and in those times when "life happens (pulled out of, can't get or stay focused)," I pull it out and put it on, get my bible, paper and pen ready to take notes. I start it again when it's time to go to bed (getting it in my spirit even when my body is resting) and start it again when I wake up. There were times in the change process when I didn't

> **Fight**: remember, speak, believe, seek God, give, receive and build yourself up!

answer the phone, didn't listen to the messages and did not turn on the TV unless it was to put "that DVD" on-again. Yes, you must get prepared for change and fight into it! In this process of changing, I knew I had to remember to constantly renew my mind with the word of God; begin to speak the word of God only and believe that it's true. Seek God daily. Give my tithes, and be a good steward over the rest. Because this is a spiritual journey. I received the baptism of the Holy Ghost, with the evidence of speaking in tongues (the perfect prayer) so that I could build myself up spiritually (Jude 20 KJV). As I began to think about "what am I here for," I thought...*love, relationships and marriage is serious; this is "Kingdom Business!" The world has tried to defame the covenant of marriage; women are walking around saying "I don't need a man!" The men walking around saying they are "scared of commitment," but living in it every day with your baby mama (that's what she's referenced as), and he is still out seeking because he knows she is not the one. Then he finds that woman that's saying she wants a husband (now he decides he's ready). She's really not sure what being a wife means. She's still too nice to ask the right questions and hasn't heard a word he is saying...., she marries him ....now she starts praying that the Lord will change him...., but what about you sister? This cycle has got to change. We must get an understanding of what it means to be a wife...a husband, according to the word of God. And you have to understand before you get married.*

I have proclaimed *change* and explained why. Now it's time to start living in it and I had to remember, it is a process! And there are levels of progression in this process. First, every decision and action that I make and take, from now on has to be based on my bottom line. My bottom line is lining my life up with the word of God. In the beginning of wanting to change, I couldn't figure out why it wasn't working? I was feeling frustrated...but I went to church anyway and this particular Sunday my pastor was teaching...and I heard him say; "things will change when you bring your life and line it up with the word of God, and stop trying to make the word of God line up to "your life." God has already set order to everything, that's why we must line our life up to His word. Lining up with the word begins with being **TRUTHFUL** (John 4:24 KJV). **Tell the truth about everything!** "I will never forget when I actually got naked before God and

"Your life;" living with a man/woman and you are not married. Or if you are married and living in it "like you are single." No, you are not going to hell for living like this, because you are saved. But there is a way Christians are to live.

when I say naked…*I actually took off all of my clothes and lay in the middle of my bedroom on the floor!* If you have to take off all your clothes, in your house, by yourself, lay in the middle of the floor, then so be it! Confess it ALL to God…the good, the bad and the ugly (1 John 1:9 KJV). Guess what? He already knows, but you must confess it to Him. Where do you start? Whatever He brings to your remembrance first, speak on it and so on. Cry…kick…scream…explain…just get it out! As you do this you will began to feel grateful, then you will began to ask for forgiveness. Most times we feel like we can't deal with the truth and/or a person "can't handle the truth," but actually they can. We were born with the truth in us, but you must speak it! There is freedom in the truth (John 8:31-36 KJV). I learned that when I'm truthful…this is the assured way of not slinging my mind back into the old way of thinking, which will eventually take my body back too. Another thing you must do to line up with the word is to study it, and refuse to go against it. ("I'm simply believing it and doing it!") No, it's not easy all the time, and there have been times I've asked God, "Hey!!" Are you there? And there have been times He has asked me the same thing! lol. This is a faith walk. Defy all of your logic and just trust Gods word…SCARED and all! Proverbs 3:5(KJV) says; "trust in the Lord with all thine heart and lean not unto my own understanding. In all my ways acknowledging Him…so that He can direct my paths…"

Now after you make the choice to go with God's way, the distractions will come. I'm talking about when the enemy reaches way back and pulls some things from one of the strongholds you **had**. Yeah, maybe that old flame, or an addiction or he might temp you with something new. When the distractions come you must stop! recognize, resist then "quickly prioritize your thoughts!" I found that I was giving too much thought to old situations. Then I took a quick trip (in my mind) down memory lane, remembered why that relationship or the situation had to end. Then asked myself, is this going to subtract from me, or add to me? Renewed my mind with the word of God, "**saying**… I am in Christ and old things have passed away; behold all things are become new (2 Corinthians 5:17 KJV), "I believe I receive God's word. It also says to "submit myself therefore to God. Resist the devil and he will flee from me." (James 4:7(KJV), Matthew 21:21-22 KJV) I "kept it moving "back to focusing on this book, school, walking into my purpose, staying in the will of God for my life.

In addition, I had to cut some people off because we weren't traveling in the same direction any more. I made sure that I was measuring all things against the word of God, asking the Holy Spirit to help me (John 14:26 & 16:13 KJV). If it doesn't line up, then I'm going to straighten it up or get rid of it, **period!** When I first started living in my change, it felt funny to keep my bottom line, it felt fearful. *Doing everything according to the word of God, speaking in faith; walking in faith; not caring that everyone else I knew had chosen to live the world's way, and I chose not to be a part of the "wrong way" anymore. It felt like I was rebelling-and I was. I had chosen to stand with the truth of my bottom line. (**This takes time to get use to, because we always want to <u>feel</u> good, and or don't want to hurt a person's feelings, instead of being honest and true to God's word first. **Do the word of God and keep reminding <u>yourself</u> that you are not living the world's way anymore.)* Change is something that we must work on every day. I keep jumping these hurdles and staying focused. Before I knew it, and before you will know it, we're living changed. Now, it's who we are!

One more thing…a big part of change is learning how to say No! Mind you, saying no makes you feel weak and a little fearful because most times you feel like you don't know how the person will handle it. We don't have to be fearful because God knows your heart and He has your back. (2 Corinthians 12:9 KJV) *This is how I say no because I know the Lord has my back:* look at the person or situation in the face, eye to eye and say no, or "I'm not doing that!" I'm saying to myself; I don't owe an explanation, it's just no. While walking away, don't say anything else and don't look back. You don't have to be rude or ugly about it. Now with some people you may have to be aggressive as you are saying NO. Don't say anything else, "Although an explanation may be lumped up in your throat trying to push its way out of your mouth, BUT DON'T SAY IT!" And when you get away from them - or it, then you can sigh, cry or scream, but don't even say the explanation to yourself… just do what?…let me hear you say it "Keep it Moving."

In conclusion, remember change doesn't happen fast or all at one time. It's a process and we have to <u>stop forcing things to happen</u>; this will cause you to operate out of order, "putting the cart before the horse." When you make things happen, you have to deal with <u>all</u> that comes with that…"suffering through"…as I call it. I know you know what I'm talking about….all the confusion…baby mama—baby daddy drama, loaning your car out, giving your money out and spending it on unnecessary things and one of the most draining things you can deal with is an indecisive person… motivating them while striving to stay motivated yourself. All those are the kinds of things that subtract from you. You should not feel obligated to stay in a situation to "be nice or, so you "won't hurt their feelings." This is not; I repeat… this is not being nice; this is lying and operating out of order. **You are not required to be nice before being obedient!** I encourage you to tell the truth niccly if you can, and remember change starts with YOU first.

CHAPTER 2

SETTING YOUR MIND FOR ETERNAL CHANGE

"Happy is the man that findeth wisdom, and the man that getteth understanding!" (Proverbs 3:13 KJV)

It is not as important to stay focused on where we came from black or white parents, a city, state or continent... **as it is to get and stay focused on what we were created for; to serve God and to do His will. His will is that every person will know Him and serve Him by way of living in the purpose He gave each one of us while in this earthly realm.**

Consider the source of your beliefs. Ask yourself, where does what I believe come from? Now you must line ALL of your beliefs up with the word of God only.

"Focus on the word of God, begin to **speak** *the word of God, then comes manifestation of the word of God-according to your faith in the word of God...by way of Jesus Christ..."*
(Genesis 1, John 14:6 KJV)

*...ask God for wisdom... and get understanding of the word of
God, also **allowing** the Holy Spirit to help you. The Holy Spirit's
help comes by way of your intuition. Most of us say..."something
told me", "my gut feeling"... or "I had an epiphany."*

*The Holy Spirit was sent to cater to **your** individual needs. He is our helper.
You have to initiate by asking the Holy Spirit to help you.
(James 1:5, Proverbs 3 and John 14:26 KJV)*

*For the ones who use the excuse "man wrote the bible, or there are
so many different versions or interpretations...how do you know for
sure?" Stop questioning the word of God and just **believe it.**
You are going to have to wait on some of the manifestations
because God doesn't operate in our time frame (the clock).
Remember, He lives in eternity where time doesn't exist.*
That's why you must believe His word! (John 1-21 KJV)

I Corinthians 13 KJV

God = Jesus, (If you believe what God said then you will follow God's way-believe and do His will first, while in the earthly realm). The nature of God is **love**, (I Corinthians 13 KJV). This is how God loves us, and how we are to love one another. He is **truth**, and to serve Him you must serve Him in spirit "**... telling the truth according to His word** (John 4:24, Psalms 26:3 KJV). Jesus came so that we can have **life and have it** more abundantly (John 10:10 KJV). He wants us to be in good health (Proverbs 3:1-8 KJV) and live in peace (Romans 8:6 KJV).

Or will you choose man = satan (if you believe what anyone else says besides the word of God then you are following the world's way). **The nature of satan is to kill, steal and destroy** (John 10:10(KJV), I John 2:15-17 KJV). You must understand, THIS IS satans only position... according to the word of God.

Now that you have chosen Christ, you must get saved/born again. This means you must confess with your mouth and believe with your heart that Jesus came, He bled and died for your sins and three days later He rose from the dead and ascended back to Heaven to be on the right hand of God, His Father. This is when He sent the Holy Spirit to live within you. John 14(KJV), / Romans 10:9-11(KJV), 2 Timothy 1:14 KJV). Start to confess the word of God and acknowledge that you believe it. Keep His commandment after Jesus came. This will draw you near to Christ, and then He will manifest himself more and more to you (John 14:21 KJV). No other knowledge comes before, or in comparison with the word of God, period! The final thing you must do is measure every decision against the word of God; <u>make it your final authority</u>. *Remember, when you ask God for something, He is not subject to our earthly time, because He is not in an earthly body.

He is a spirit and His timing is based on eternity. His thoughts are not our thoughts and His ways are not our ways (Isaiah 55:8-9 KJV). We must stop thinking He is going to solve an issue the way we want Him to solve it. This is what you must do: STOP!...for about five minutes, get by yourself and get quiet, take about three deep breaths, close your eyes and focus. Speak "now Lord you said in your word, in Proverbs 3:5(KJV) (open the bible and read it out loud) "Trust in the Lord... and lean not to my own understanding...In all thy ways..." Then ask Him for wisdom (James 1:5 KJV). Now you must do what He said do. In most situations you will see or learn, while you were taking five minutes out of your way God has already solved it or has the situation under control. This is a part of renewing your mind with the word of God and getting in alignment with His word. God is a God of order and He will not go outside of the order He has set for us. God's word is absolute! It's complete! Whatever question and answer you need is in the bible. The last thing that we must settle...you must know the definition of Love...according to the word of God.

CHAPTER 3

THE TRUE DEFINITION OF LOVE

(John 15:9-17 KJV)

I Corinthians 13 KJV

Almighty Love! We are always in search of it, consciously or unconsciously looking for it everywhere we go and in everything we do. Love is always present. When we come in contact with it we are afraid to allow ourselves to identify with it, probably because the word "love" has been used so much as a pawn for selfish gain. I believe If we understood exactly **"what love looks like"** (I Corinthians 13 KJV), and began to operate in it ourselves, it would be easier to identify. "The foundation of love is giving, **"give what you want"** (Matthew 7:12 KJV). There are two words that best describe giving, **to serve.** The condition of your heart (the good or the evil residing within your heart) will determine why and how you serve (Luke 6:45 KJV). It is this simple to understand love.

I Corinthians 13(KJV) explains' how Christ **loves us.** He commanded us to **love** the way He does (John 13:34 KJV). How do you come to the point of experiencing love so that you can give it? First, you must believe and acknowledge the definition of love according to the source from which it was created...God. The first three verses of I Corinthians 13(KJV) say's, "even though you can speak with tongues of men...., ...prophecy, understand mysteries, have faith that can remove mountains, ...feed the poor, or give your body to be burned, and have not **love,** these things profit you NOTHING." WOW! Verses 4-7(KJV) explain how to **love**, what **love** does, its characteristics, the dos and don'ts of loving, what love looks like, and how it feels. I call this section **"The course of actions to love."** Verses 8-13(KJV) tell us love never fails, **nothing can compete with love,** prophecies, tongues shall cease and knowledge will disappear. For now we know "love" in part...but when that which is perfect is come...that which is in part shall be done away. When we were children, we acted as children, but now that we are mature we should no longer act immature.

While on earth we are able to experience love in part, but in heaven we will experience love in full…faith, hope, love…but the greatest of these is Love!

I believe when you began to understand and operate in "**the course of *actions to love,***" we will see the effects of it in every relationship that is a part of our lives!

Love is patient.- Patient means to be in no hurry, able to accept the person and/or tolerate delays. The word suffer is not to be taken as a burden. It means "to compromise, go through, to put up with." There is no time limit on being patient in the **covenant of marriage.** Why? because God sees you as one. The same patience you take for yourself is the same patience you will give to your spouse. This is one of the first priorities for marriage. **This is why being equally yoked (believing the same, according to the word of God) will definitely make this easier. This is something you need to know before you take the vows… "remember….this is forever"** (James 1:3-5(KJV), Genesis 2:18-24 KJV). I must say…learning to be patient is not always easy, but if you shift your focus (just for a moment) and **listen** to what that person is saying, which is what they believe to be true, then you can begin to understand them more. Now you can make an informed decision. Will you continue a friendship or will you need to distance yourself so that you are not taken out of the will of God for your life?

Love is kind. Love in action! Actions display kindness, your look (facial expressions), the way you speak (your tone), and in your giving and receiving (Eph. 4:32(KJV), Luke 6:35 KJV).

Love does not envy. What are you **irritated** by? Someone else's achievements/happy they didn't achieve their goals? If you find yourself focused on **competing** with a person and that is all you think about, you are envious. Competition promotes jealousy, and ends in resentment, which is hard to recover from. Or, if you are **criticizing** and calling it "I'm just telling the truth," examine yourself, quick! Criticism doesn't move people in to action; it makes them mean and mad. And if you are fueled by criticism…yes you will achieve it!...but look who you have become (operating with a vengeance mindset) in the process of trying to prove something to someone who doesn't even care, or/and you were the furthest thing from their mind! (Proverbs 6:34-35(KJV), 2 Cor. 13:5-14 KJV)

Love does not boast. -Have an attitude of humility. Don't let pride take over you. Boasting will cause you to be a "show off," or have you driven to prove something.

Love is not proud/prideful. Pride has the face of self-confidence, the stance of an Amazon, and actions of the thief! Pride steals your purpose, it will kill the spirit and it will eventually destroy it-self! Proverb 13:10, Proverbs 16:18 Being prideful won't allow you to be able to receive, and you must be able to receive in relationships. This will also give the giver an opportunity to receive as well, when you let the pride go!

Love is not rude. Don't be offensive. How do you know if someone is offended? You will notice an instant change in their attitude towards you. They will stop talking and/or sometimes knowingly or unknowingly take an open opportunity to make a "smart remark" to you. Sometimes they may even say something that they know will upset you Most times, when a person offends someone they know they have. We have become a people that lean on "well, I'm just telling the truth." It's best to tell the truth, but it doesn't have to be offensive. Rudeness is a main problem starter in relationships, and 9 times out of 10 the offense is often ingested but never digested, and becomes an ulcer. Every time an ulcer is hit with anything spicy (offending again), it's irritated!! The only way to solve and recover from being rude is to **"always do unto others as you would have them do unto you (Matthew 7:12 KJV)," I call this scripture the cure all! If we could just continually come back to this scripture, so many of our issues would be solved.**

Love is not self-seeking. Being a self seeker is a matter of the heart, and based in fear. Most times self-seekers fear someone will take something from them and/or them not getting something back in return for their giving. Self seekers rarely give without a reason, and often feel bad about receiving. Why? Because they know what they are receiving is something they wouldn't give. To conquer this, "be the giver". Learn how to accept/believe and you will learn to give/provide. "...give and it shall be given unto you; good measure, pressed down, and shaken together, and running over, shall men give into your bosom. For with the same measure that ye mete (that you give), withal-(in addition), it shall be measured to you again" (Luke 6:30-38 KJV). **Note:** This action may not come back from the person you are giving it to. Just trust the word of God; it will come back to you.

Love is not easily angered. Why are you easily angered? Fear! Fear makes you automatically defensive. Defense has the face of anger. Then we start to speak while in this frame of mind, and it doesn't turn out good most of the time. This can be changed if you immediately recognize the anger in you. Question yourself. Why am I afraid? Be honest with yourself; own your part in the reason why. This course of action will require "you to work on it." **Note:** Don't let "working on it" become an excuse that takes you years to get to the point of really changing. If you truly work on it, change comes and it will stay!

Love keeps no record of wrongs. Forgiveness! You must forgive. Do you understand what that truly means? **I like to say it like this, "Give what you want."** If you want to be forgiven you must forgive, asked of you or not. I have heard so many people say "that's a deal breaker or, that's unforgiveable! I can't forgive that." Any time you feel like this, examine yourself first. Yes, God has given everyone the ability to forgive. That person may not have done the same as you have done, but you have done something that you have or should have asked forgiveness for (Matthew 6:14-15 KJV).

Love does not delight in evil but rejoices with the truth. *Not delighting in evil* is self-explanatory (Proverbs 17:23 KJV), but I have to say this, so that you will truly get it. When you choose to be a part of anything or any situation, there are only two ways to choose from. Good or bad, evil or righteous, God's way or the world's way. Please know there is no grey area. There is no fence to be on, no in the middle. Make a decision! Making a decision to not do the right thing (according to the word of God), in the name of "love or helping someone," doesn't mean a thing in God's eyes. He will forgive you, but on the other side – in the world's eyes, you are an accessory to the crime/situation, and you will have to pay with your time and/or money. Choose life! Always choose to be righteous and to tell the truth because this is God's way. Not your truth or what "mama-them" said, but the truth "thus saith the Lord." **Do not compromise the truth for the sake of anything!** (Proverbs 3:3 KJV) Now you know this is where we go and say "God will understand." Not at all! Always focus on telling the truth. (Proverbs 91:4).

Love bears all things. This means to be accountable, to cover, always making sure that the <u>truth is represented and demonstrated</u>. Put on the breast plate of righteousness every day (Ephesians 6:10-17/Proverbs 3:3-4 KJV).

Love never loses trust. Always believe, and have confidence in the truth. We must remember to confess, I walk by faith and not by sight (Ephesians 3:12 KJV).

Love always hopes. Be eager to believe for the best. Have good expectations always!

Love always perseveres. Be persistent, constant and keep on **believing in love!**

CHAPTER 4

EFFECTIVE COMMUNICATION

(Proverbs 18 KJV)

I Corinthians 13 KJV

Understanding how to communicate effectively is vital to your entire life! You've heard the saying, "you can get more bees with honey than with vinegar, right?" It's true. There are ways to communicate with worth and disposition, which shows the person you care, respect and/or love them. The way you communicate can tear a person down, make them defensive or help build them up (Proverbs 17:22 KJV). Knowing how, what, or when to say or not to say something at all is important to the intimacy and assurance wanted and needed in a relationship. Knowing how to ask, answer, and react is what I call:

> ## "Honey do ism"

I truly believe your words should be felt without you touching the person, but instead of it feeling like a jab, make your words feel like strokes of kindness. One way of relating to this, when we speak to a person most times we want to get back a positive answer, response or we want to hear "yes…" or even when the answer is no, it's better if you *"give~~~"* the no, and not **"throw------"** the no. A person will be more inclined to deal with your answer better. One of the best ways to get what you want is to **give what you want…period! (Matthew 7:12 KJV)**

Instead of putting yourself in a position to have to apologize, explain and then have to stroke them with those same words you could have used in the beginning, let's work on starting there. Every action will get a reaction of some kind. Who do you want to talk to or deal with, "The King or The Queen" or would you like to deal with "the Fool or the Crazy

Girl?" Trust me, the way you ask, answer, or react will determine who you will bring forth!

Learn, practice, and always use yes, please, and thank you! When your name is called; while turning to acknowledge the call, answer with yes (kind-a singing it). Please and thank you go hand in hand. But don't run them together....then it becomes sarcastic! If you are asked a question and you agree, answer "yes," or please~ listen to the rest of what the person is saying and then say, thank you. These words are the win-win words in communicating. I like to relate communicating to creating beautiful music! Ladies always remember you "set the tone" for your relationship... no matter where you are or what you're doing. If you come home slamming doors, huffing and puffing, you have just set or just changed the tone in your home. Everybody will separate and go to their neutral corners. Your tone will dictate the sound of "your music." Men, you own the melody. Your melody will give her music harmony. Then there's the vamp of the music. The vamp is better known as the chorus. You know the chorus of a song is the part that resonates in you. When you hear this particular song you get excited, start dancing and saying turn it up! If you haven't heard that song in a while, or something or a situation reminds you of it, "but you can't remember the words," you're searching your memory and saying... "hold on...it's on the tip of my tongue, wait a minute...it's gone come to me." We're waiting...you're dancing, snapping your fingers... "there comes one word!" You are bobbing your head and all of a sudden you shout the rest of the words! You know what I'm talking about? So let your communication began to resonate! So much so, that when your family hears it they began to groove~~ (husband and children will know they can open up with you) to it Because you sound so good! I encourage you to make your communication a piece of music that your family would

> *QUICK EXERCISE:*
> *Look at yourself in the mirror, smile.......*
> *go ahead do it, and say—yes, please, thank you. Men, you do it too. Men, I know you are saying I'm not smiling at myself, but say it in a moderate tone of voice. If your tone is too high you sound funny, and if too low it sounds too macho. Work on that, and see how it works. I can guarantee you the responses you get back will be great!!*

always want to hear and/or play. Not only will your family want to play your music, your co-workers and everyone you communicate with will too! It will become infectious! Men, please understand "what you just said" will be directly <u>connected</u> to her feelings, especially when she has the "googly eyes" for you. That's why your melody (the way you communicate with her) is so important. Giving is also a form of communicating with her. Visiting empty handed? Don't. Bring her something when you know you are going to see her, or ask is something is needed. If bringing something is not feasible for you (in the beginning), is there something that needs to be fixed? What does her lawn look like? Yassss... I think you've got it! Men, women were created to move "to your rhythm." You must be sure to make your rhythm look and sound good. This is how she begins to trust you, and once you gain her trust "she will reverence your rhythm forever." I was talking to a client of mine, and she began to tell me one thing, and out of nowhere she began to say..."I love it when my husband makes me feel like I am the only person in the world that matters to him. "He can get anything from me." Learn how to do this and instantly your relationship will change forever!

Men: there are **two more things** that will help establish your rhythm. 1. **<u>Tune your ears to her.</u>** This will keep you knowledgeable, so that you understand her better. If there is ever something you don't know or understand, ask her. (*Ladies, when he asks, please answer him the way you would like to be answered). 2. **<u>Control your eyes.</u>** This will help you to have control over your thoughts. "This knowledge will be your Power." Know that the woman is waiting on the right melody for her tone.

Communicating has to do with the condition of the heart. "For out of the abundance of the heart does the mouth speak." (Matthew 12:34 KJV) <u>Give what you want</u>. (Luke 6:31 KJV) Speak to a person the way you would like to be spoken to (Colossians 3:23-25 KJV). The chart at the end of this chapter was created to give you some new or alterative words to use when you begin to speak, ask, answer or close a statement or conversation. Did you ever think about a closing? It's a good thing to open and close a conversation on a good note. This invites more conversation because of the positive impact that has occurred. Closing a conversation or discussion will help to eliminate misunderstandings. Also, your ability to receive an opening and a closing helps a person to deliver a decision better. "Yes" is better than yeah. Saying "yes" doesn't mean that you are agreeing to something; it's the tone of your voice that you use with the "yes."

> *QUICK EXERCISE: You have to lighten up your tone of voice. Men too, when I say light I mean the way it will feel to you. Try this: raise your eyebrows, which gives you a feeling of lightness and it "kind of" make you feel bright, and creates a semi-smile. Take a deep breath and move your eyes from left to right about two or three times. I know that sounds crazy, but it works! Then you will begin your opening words...pause...this will get the other persons attention, then proceed to talk.*

Don't let a person's negative reaction change how or what you were going to say. It can be discouraging if their response isn't "right" in the beginning. But if you keep opening with words that enhance or encourage, that person will start to do the same and/or receive better, even when they've had a crazy day...lol.

Listening is equally as important as speaking. In James 1:19-20(KJV), it says, "wherefore, my beloved brethren, let every man be swift to hear, slow to speak, and slow to wrath: (20), for the wrath of man worketh not the righteousness of God." Most times we are quick to "think we know" the rest of what a person has started to say, but when you listen quickly you actually miss what is being said. Because you "think" (assume) you know, you stop listening and cut them off. In the midst of cutting them off, you lie and say "I don't mean to cut you off, but..." so now the person is upset and they start to talk louder in an effort to be heard. Now you are talking louder and it turns into hollering. All of a sudden the subject changes because you're mad and then comes old unresolved issues. This can get crazy!! **NOTE:** If something from the past comes up in an argument that means the person has not truly gotten over it and let it go. It has turned into resentment; one of you must start the conversation to get this ***RESOLVED IMMEDIATELY! If you don't, your relationship will start to take some unnecessary hits. That can be fatal—as in the spiritual death of your relationship.*** (Proverbs 18 KJV) You must practice being an **active listener**; swift to hear. Turn to the person, look at them, and force yourself to stay quiet. If you don't understand the first time because you were trying to get focused, just ask them "say it again please?" Then process what you just heard. Being slow to speak will cause fewer wraths. It will stop a person from "flying off the handle before they have a chance to understand what's being said. This will take your ability to be an active listener to the next level. Yeah!...you're getting better! **Speaking**: when you are speaking to someone, make it plain! *It's not right to speak in deception*—telling the person a lie with gestures and voice tones to convince them you are speaking the truth. The same concept applies when you're speaking the truth! We tell the truth, but we have this way of telling the truth, then saying something afterwards to make light of it so we "won't hurt someone's feelings or make the person feel bad." The truth is, you already made them feel bad, because the truth doesn't always feel good when you first hear it. Instead of making light of the truth, it's best to simply say "Ok, I'll talk to you later...hang up and/or walk away. Then, when you talk later, stand on the truth. *The truth can be spoken with kindness, and if you have to, speak it KIND AND LOUD!! IT'S OK. JUST SPEAK THE TRUTH!!* Oh and not responding, becoming silent, is not the way to communicate! Be truthful from the beginning and then you won't have to use silence as a message.

What **offends** a person the most? Most times it's not what's said about them, it's the way it's said to them. I've found that most people are offended if you say "anything" to them. Why are we so offended? Why so touchy? Where does that come from? It's ok for a person to ask a question without us automatically getting offended or thinking something is wrong. When you ask for an opinion or give one, it's just that, if it's not based on the word of God. Criticism has a lot to do with why we are so offended. Criticism is a trick of the enemy. It's his way of distracting you and/or putting you in bondage. When you become bound up by criticism you become consumed with the criticism, and now you become unproductive, in that area.

> Criticizing is not the way to get someone to understand that they should change. That never works because it hurts. Next, there will be resentment.

Remember that saying…"sticks and stones may break my bones, but words will never hurt me?" I'm not sure who started telling that lie, but that is so far from the truth! Proverbs 23:16 (KJV) says; "Yea, my **reins** shall rejoice, when thy lips speak right things." Your **reins/**your loins are considered to be the place of your emotions and affections. Offensive words, criticism and the lack of hearing encouraging and enhancing words make it hard for a person to progress in any type of relationship. Most times your words have the ability to balance the whole situation. (Proverbs 15:4 KJV) That's why **we must not offend or criticize**. If you do, please fix it immediately! We were always told to watch what we say in an argument because we may say something we didn't mean. Not true, because when you are mad, you say exactly what you mean, because you have been holding the truth in; "trying to spare their feelings..." that's lying and it keeps them and you from being free!

In conclusion: This is the way I have learned to communicate effectively in every situation and under any circumstance. When I'm being spoken to **I give my undivided attention,** and just like I told you earlier in this chapter, **I force myself to listen** (because one of the things I did not like about my "past-self" is that I would cut people off and start speaking what I'm thinking…that was horrible!) **and after I've heard them**…most times I ask questions because I need to be sure that I understand what they mean before I answer, if I answer. I do not answer according to what I think or by the way I'm feeling…EVER! I say back to you

> "the heart of the prudent getteth knowledge; and the ear of the wise seeketh knowledge, Proverbs 18:15(KJV)

what you said to me then I answer truthfully and relating the answer to the word of God. Let me say to all of you who are saying she is too deep…I really have learned to answer according to what the word of God says. I truly do this for myself and have seen time and time again that it works in my life. Let's not continue to go to church and proclaim we are Christians and not go to the word of God for our answers. We must do it, ALWAYS! (Ephesians 4:15-32 KJV).

The chart below contains words of enhancement and encouragement to help you communicate better so that you can keep the lines of communication open in your relationships. Some of the words and quotes may be a little "buttery", but that's a good thing.

The "Honey-do-ism" Chart				
Opening	**Ask**	**Answer**	**React**	**Closing**
Honey	Is it ok	Yes	I don't understand	Thank You
Baby	Would you mind	Yes my love	Please, Honey Let's talk	Sweetheart, I love you (smile)
Lovie	I would like you to..	Certainly Dear	Look Sweetly	You make me happy
Sweetchums	Honey, I need you to..	Yes Honey	*	Thank You for loving me
Honey? I'm suggesting	Baby please help me (as you are extending your hand)	Yes, Thank you	Touch the Hand or the Back	I love the way you show me that you love me, baby.
Excuse me baby	It would be great if…	Yes, Please	Kiss them Softly	You are so handsome/ beautiful to me, baby.
You know, I was thinking about… Or Honey I would like to talk., Is this a good time?	*	Thank you Honey, but I've decided to…	Embrace with no Patting	Oh Honey (as you are reaching over to hug or kiss him/her)

*Fill in something you would say.

CHAPTER 5

DATING TO MARRIAGE

Dating…a systematic approach into a lifelong commitment.

In this chapter we will redefine the way we date…into marriage!

First, we will Pre-date;

If you do this then you can make a decision to stop here or go further.

PLEASE DO NOT skip this part or move through it faster than recommended.

Then a mutual decision must be made to date into marriage,
then you will date and get to know each other (building a friendship),
then you get engaged,
now we talk about the money! *(We don't talk money before the engagement, and you do not combine bank accounts or exchange information until after the wedding).*

I Corinthians 13 KJV

Dating to Marriage! I say…this is the chapter where "you got to get your mind right…again!" I'm going to tell you like I tell myself and my friends; we are not jumping into another relationship without thinking it out step by step, all the way through into marriage. This is what we do now: *New mindset* – say it… "Now I **"Pre-date first."** So…you just met someone and you "like what you hear, enough to exchange phone numbers." Now this is where you need to be honest with yourself – be honest with yourself to know if you are ready to start **talking** to someone with the intent to develop a friendship that could lead to marriage. In this **pre-dating phase talking on the phone is all you will do.** And, you will have

> **The Only Pre-dating rules:**
>
> ****No phone call before 10am and none after 10pm. Yes…at 10pm say goodnight…and no texting.**

to remind yourself of this on many occasions. LOL….there is nothing wrong with you. While you are in this body you will have to bring it and sometimes beat it into subjection…make it do what the word of God says to do. Did someone say how? The body is programmable because it works on memory. If you constantly give it sugar, bacon, going out on a date before it's time, kissing, sex…that's what it will crave. LOL…yes, I went there, so you will not be confused. If you stop giving your body something for about seven to ten days, it will start to calm down. You will go through withdrawals but don't try any substitutes. Just be persistent. Then for the next seven to ten days it will be easier to just talk on the phone. It seems like I went to left field, but trust me, your past routine will try to take over! God has a "code of behavior" for entering into marriage. I say marriage here, because after **pre-dating** we should decide to **date** with the intent to marry. If you don't want to get married, you shouldn't start a dating relationship.

When the Lord gave me this revelation about dating into marriage, I was in the middle of a relationship where we went from meeting straight into consummating. With new revelation, I was trying to figure out how I was going to turn it around, and he was wondering why all of the changes so suddenly! Eventually we broke up. For all of my optimistic people reading this

---

The order of a relationship, that's evolving into marriage.

Boy finds girl, —sparks fly. They talk on the phone for a while.

A mutual agreement is made to date with the purpose of getting married.

They date. He asks for her hand in Marriage. She accepts.

They get engaged and set a date. They Marry and

consummate after the Marriage!

---

saying what if he was the one?" At one point I thought that too, and he had potential, but he wasn't trying to hear my heart about doing things according to the word of God. **Oh Well!**, became my stance. I, too, am **very** optimistic, but I couldn't keep hanging on hoping his potential would become what I needed. That was not good enough. I needed to see action that produced results...**period!** Allowing men to be in your life with just potential will only make them lazier and more unproductive. They don't want to be that way nor do they like it. **But** if we allow them to just be the man with potential, that's just what they will be. Men, if you are feeling "some-kind-a-way" about what I just said, take a good look at yourself, from the prospective of what the word of God says about you becoming a husband. (Chapter 6 KJV)

Ladies, meeting someone and going straight into consummating is why we automatically start to operate with the **commitment mindset**. That's how we end up slinging them into our lives, becoming sympathetic to their issues and giving our all "to help them." No longer can we give too much, too soon. Remember, we are the determining factor. When we say yea it has to mean yea and when we say nay it has to definitely stay nay. (Matthew 5:37 KJV) Please stop thinking we can be "just friends" when we meet a man. If you are not ready to **exchange your single life for a married life** then stay focused on your purpose until you are ready. Did someone say "Oh, so we can't have friends of the opposite sex?" Can you? Most times when we call ourselves being "just friends," you end up crossing the boundaries and eventually breaking all the rules. When you start spending time with this person, you will become attached. Emotionally first, and the more time you spend with them you will become physically attached too, now you're having sex. Automatically your expectation level changes," and eventually you will want more than sex. Trust me, **the more point** always comes. Right there is where the problems really begin. When you start wanting more...you have got to go back in your mind and recollect what the agreement was, if there was one...! There was no agreement because you are just friends...right? You still ignore what you know, thinking you can change or help him make up his mind, but you can't. You become frustrated. He gives in and you get married under pretense... "you're pregnant?" Now you both are raising a baby in this forced marriage, you are both stressed out; the baby sees all of this, but you decide to stay and get along "for the sake of the child?" You just added another confused person to the world who is out here searching for "love." **No more! Let's just date in order.** No friends with benefits! Also remember ladies, men don't get frustrated about having sex

> *Oh!...and there is nothing honorable about living a lie.*

outside of wedlock as easily as we do. *I'm not saying it's right, but you need to understand if you allow him to be in a relationship and have sex with you before the commitment, then you are <u>setting yourself up to be hurt</u>. (Hurt means you received a different result from what you thought the <u>result would be</u>). There is no need to want to fall off the map or not participate in a relationship again. Own your mistakes; read, believe and do what the word of God says and by yourself. These three things will get you on or back on track!* Ladies remember, men were made to find their wives, and they know instantly most of the time when they've found her! If he feels like you're his wife, his responses will be totally different toward you. He'll be nervous and most times scared to say something wrong. Oh but he'll never admit that he's scared, but trust me he will find a way to get the right words out of his mouth. If you are not "the one," he will not claim you and you will not be his priority. A lot of us have been in denial too long trying to figure him out. If you are "waiting for him to get ready for marriage," after two or three years of dating, you are probably not the one. And you shouldn't keep waiting. And certainly don't ask him or imply anything about marriage, *(tell yourself the truth-because you really already know you are not the one for him and you are not satisfied either).* If you feel like you have to ask him…Oh well (take the stance), and keep it moving. One of the most important things I have learned…**"honey….you don't want nobody…who don't want you!"** Yeah…I know that's a big-ole horse pill to swallow, but chew it on up…lol. It might take you a month to swallow it all, but get it down baby so you can "keep it moving!"

Stay with me ladies… remember this; we are not equal to men and we weren't made to be. And they were not made to be equal to us. This is the way I describe it; men are ABC people, and women are D thru Z people. If you ask him to do anything other than get a career/job/build a business, build you a house, possess and protect it, he's lost (Genesis 2:15 KJV). After he does those things we are to help him grow/multiply and maintain what the Lord has brought him here to do (Proverbs 31). When you meet someone and decide to date, make sure you are listening to what he is saying! He is going to tell you what he believes. Don't think you can change him, that's

> The word of God says, "…out of the abundance of the heart, does the mouth speak!" (Luke 6:45 KJV)

not for you to do. Why would you want to? Watch the way he treats other people…and you (in that order). If you do these two things you will hear and see **everything** you need to know! Listening and watching is the key to finding out exactly who he is. Remember, this is the man who could be the head of your household. Keep in mind, when you say those vows, in his mind he is saying she agrees and understands who I am. If you don't **like** who he is, he is probably not the one. "Don't under estimate liking your potential spouse. **You need to like him!**

So lets' assume you got through the **pre-dating** phase and you both have decided that you like each other enough to make an agreement to date only each other. This will give you an opportunity to develop a friendship. Now these are the **rules and the boundaries** for pre-dating and dating. They are important to have because they will help lower the risk of having sex before marriage. I'm not sugarcoating this. To have sex before marriage is out of order. Also, it's one of the biggest problems in dating along with not being totally honest. **The boundaries...maybe** you can adjust some of the boundaries after a period of dating. Make them realistic (*you know what you will and won't do*), but don't change or break the **rules**! <u>YOU</u> should follow them, and not necessarily *speak them*. I say this, because when YOU follow the rules and don't cross the boundaries, what choice does the other person have but to accept what YOU allow or don't allow, right? Right. They will either fall in line or get out of the line. And if he/she chooses to get out of the line, the first thing you will hear is that favorite quote (ladies most likely) "I'm a grown... man." I don't have time for this! Or "we are adults!" Oh, and my personal favorite, "why are you punishing yourself?...lol." Don't believe the "SCARE tactic!" It's just BLUFF!" YES, this will have you feeling like you have to prove yourself, and/or it will make you feel childish. GET OVER IT! That's what we are doing, "putting away childish things and becoming a man!" (I Corinthians 13:11) On this journey the Lord has "checked me" about quoting clichés and agreeing with people when I don't... just to appease them. Then saying "Lord, please forgive me. I didn't want to hurt their feelings or be confrontational." When you are confronted with the "BLUFF," don't just go along with them to make them think you are "down with it," when you're not! This amounts to telling a lie. We have to **BE** truthful at all times! No, it's not easy to be truthful when you have been taught to be "nice." **Being nice doesn't come before being obedient.**

**The rules and boundaries are meant to slow you down, so you can think before you act. If you follow them you will learn so much about each other on your way into marriage. **

THE RULES

1. <u>Always</u> renew your mind to operate "decent and in order".
2. Be truthful at all times, while speaking it with kindness (your tone).
3. Before making any decisions, be honest with yourself about your motives.
    Men - know why you are pursuing?
    Women - know why you are accepting /allowing?
4. Absolutely No physical contact!
5. Do not date more than one person at a time.
6. ***DO NOT TEXT.*** **Talk on the phone for 10 to 20 days before setting a first date. Literally 10 to 20 days.** This may take 30 days, count the days if you need to. If the person doesn't fit and you decide to move forward, or if they feel that way about you too, Great! This simply means they are not the one and its ok, because we have no time to waste. Remember, you just met this person; you are getting to know them, **you owe them nothing and they owe you nothing**
7. Wait at least 30 days before pursing or accepting.

These rules may seem strict, but there are other things going on in your separate lives that are priority over dating...work, church and you must stay focused on your purpose in life. If you don't know...ask the Holy Spirit, accept it and get working on it.

Strive not to talk about past relationships...as in dwelling on it.

Asking Questions? Ask relevant questions...as in where you are in the getting to know each other process.

Example: How much a person makes is not relevant in the pre-dating phase. Learning about who they are is more important.

Your conversation should be respectful at all times. For the ones that I need to go there for, "do not talk about sex or sexual subjects. *In the pre-dating, getting to know each other stage, is not the arena for that.*

BUT, if and when those times occur and you start to feel "the Fire" (raging hormones) that means IT'S TIME TO GO! GET OUT OF THERE AND RUN!!!

(Just save yourself)

"I put emotions in the category with the natural things you can't control: the Wind, Rain, Ice and Fire. When activated, "TAKE COVER!"...

THE BOUNDARIES

1. **Phone Calls: no phone calls before 10am or after 10pm.**
2. Always plan and then <u>meet</u> at a public place. <u>Inside</u> of a restaurant, coffee shop, book store. Sit across from each other.

<u>DO NOT meet inside of any type of vehicle.</u> Drive separate Cars.

DO NOT go to the movie theater, in the beginning of dating.

(You are not in the dating phase until a decision is made that you arc a couple committing to Date into Marriage.)

NEVER go to <u>any one's</u> house.

NEVER meet at any family, work or church functions.

This will allow you to get to know each other before introducing the person to your family and friends.

3. Dates are to be 1 to 2 hours.
4. All dates should be planned and should end before 10pm. **No exceptions!**
5. No more than 2 dates a week. After 16 weeks, 3 dates' a week, and no more than 4hrs a date.

***Talking before 10am** -Starting your day is intimate, you're organizing and getting your mind right to handle the day. They don't need to know that kind of information until you make a decision that they are the one you will date into marriage. **Talking after 10pm** puts you in a more vulnerable position to talk about sex. By this time you have wound down and your ability to think consciously has probably wound down too...

***You must take this seriously.** *Caution:* It's important to be honest with yourself first about what you are feeling if "you are feeling sexy/sexual," and if it is weighing heavily on you...my advice is for you not to be around the person or have any conversation (that day). If you ever end a date early, or a phone conversation – for this reason, do not talk, text or see each other for the rest of the evening. Wait until the next day or two.

This may seem petty, but this is crucial!! Self-control is so important.

DATING

Ladies and gentlemen if you are single, why are you living like you're married?

No more playing house. **"STOP IT NOW!"** This is the only way to gain control of this situation. It's so out of control that we have begun to believe "that's just the way it is." **No it's not! Forgive yourself; believe again, and let's live in a way that is pleasing to God.**

Now that you both have agreed to date with the intent to marry, now what? Be yourself and have fun? You must think about what "fun" means to you. I think you'll be fine, as long as "fun" doesn't mean throwing your hands up and "just letting it all hang out!" Or like they say, "When in Rome...we do what the Romans do!" Or my personal favorite, "what happens in Vegas stays in Vegas. We all know what these phrases mean," go with the flow." We are not just going with the flow-of the world-anymore, that's what got us in this mess! From now on we are making **conscious decisions**, according to the word of God. I know you may be thinking... in dating? Absolutely! The first thing we will start to do as we embark on this "new way of thinking while dating, is acknowledging Him in all our ways and He will direct our paths (Proverbs 3:5-7 KJV). *Always remember, "...at the end of the day, "you should know and do*

Steps to making a Conscious Decision:

Before you make any decision:
1. **"Be clear,"** ask questions, get an understanding of each question, situation and/or circumstance. **Do not assume anything!**
(Proverbs 4:6-8 KJV)
2. **Pray** – Ask for discernment.
(Proverbs 3:5, Joshua 1:5 KJV)

3. **"Stop and think it out."** It takes about 3 to 5 minutes. Don't allow yourself or anyone to rush you into making a decision.

   3a. Prioritize what you just heard; (as a matter of importance/accountable for you)
-**Important** –this will immediately affect my life.
-**Important but not urgent** – can be dealt with later.
-**How will this decision** add or subtract from me at this time?
Note: If you ever feel indecisive at the time of trying to make a decision, don't make one. Simply come back to it later.

what the word of God says about everything."**Also the rules and the boundaries will help guide you while dating.

Now we must talk about how to recognize your prospective spouse and being equally yoked. You should also know that it is ok to resolve issues differently…and much more. Are you ready? It's time to get naked. Maybe I should say transparent! In order for you to begin to transform your thinking into dating in the way that is pleasing to God, it's going to take nakedness! Naked simply means recognizing what **the truth** is about you and then telling it to you first. The whole truth! The more you begin to tell you the truth – according to the word of God that is…it will be easier to recognize. (John 4:24 (KJV), John 8:31-32 (KJV), Romans 6:18 KJV)

CHOP! CHOP! LADIES

While I'm saying chop chop ladies…I'm clapping my hands and throwing my head up-with the dignified look on my face! No longer are we going to be out of the will of God, playing house! From now on we are going to remember that we are the determining factor! **You determine** if you are ready for the responsibility of a relationship **before you give** him any of your **time**….or your **help!** After you decide that it's time to spend time getting to know him, don't put yourself in a position to give him one of the main benefits… sex. That should only be given after he marries you! Lately I've noticed a lot of emphasis has been put on abstaining from sex and/or announcing that this is what you are doing. These conversations had the connotation-like they are making the ultimate sacrifice or like they are going to be rewarded by God and/or honored by others because they waited! **There is no reward or honor to get. This is what we are supposed to do anyway, according to the word of God!** So let's get and stay humble about this part of lining up with the word. Oh! And as far as you helping him…the Lord is a present help and the best help he could ever get! (Psalms 46:1) We are making no more excuses Ladies!

Also ladies, while we think we can get in a marriage and stay independent (self-governing), we cannot. I said marriage and not relationship because they are not the same. A relationship means connected by association, marriage is a lifelong commitment. We must stop intertwining these two meanings in our thinking, and start to "expand our understanding to accommodate this truth-according to the word of God." (Proverbs 4:7-9 KJV) Ladies, you must understand that your independence doesn't end when you get married. Its position of power changes because you are no longer single. You must relinquish the throne. Now, you must talk to your husband, who is the head of your household, when there is a decision to be made about ALL things. Knowing when and how to use our independence shows you are listening to what he has to say and you **respect it.** (Ephesians 5:33 KJV) When you do this he will tell you everything. Ladies, we are the help meet. He needs the natural help that God supplied us with for him.

This is the most important attribute of our independence. (The perfect example is Proverbs 31 KJV)

The women's liberation era, men taking advantage of their authority along with us not knowing what is required of us to be a wife and not listening to our intuition, has a lot to do with why we have been so challenged in our thinking about our God given dependency for the man. We are making more money than most men, buying our own houses and cars. We boast about "not needing a man!" And" if he doesn't have what I have...," we are looking down at him while still dealing with him but in a "conniving kind-a way." Now, we are getting the backlash from being "too independent," but still "at the end of the day" it's in us to be "dependent" on him. No longer can we think we can hold on to our "independence" with one hand, while hiding the other—tooting our butts in the air getting part of his "dependence." Yeah, I said it because it's true. Also, we are always trying to make him measure up to "our independent qualities, but it will never work, because God did not make him to do what we can do. This is one of the main reasons for the breakdown of the family structure. I'm certainly not B-rating our independence, because without it a lot more children and families would be lost. I'm not advocating "taking excuses or agreeing to less than what you need...to be married." But you must understand it is vital to know how and when to use your independence in your marriage. This is one of the main ingredients in the glue that will help hold our marriages together for 60 and 70 years.

MEN...STAY FOCUSED AND MAKE NO EXCUSES

Men, meeting "the one" can take some time, but be patient and pay attention! We live in a world where lies have become the "norm." We are not living the world's way anymore. We are living God's way and that is telling the truth and living in it, according to the word of God (John 4:24 KJV).

Every woman you meet does not need to experience your goodness in full, first. Yes, I'm addressing the stigma that has been put on men." You can't wait, you've just got to have sex," "men are physical first." This is learned behavior. We, Christian men and women, are expected to know that we are to do all things decent and in order, because we're representing Christ. Renew your mind by keeping the word of God in your mouth. This will help you while you insist that she waits to have sex until after marriage. Meanwhile men, while women are busy learning to be virtuous women, don't get lazy, or shall I say "**stop being lazy**!"

Pursuing is a man's job. I've heard men give the excuse (violins playing) about being turned down, being rejected, and they were wounded to the point of them being scared to pursue again. "Well, at least not as fast as they use to." *Ladies, NOT SO! Not only have I experienced "the pursuits," I did some research on it too. It is a known fact, that when a man is interested in YOU...honey when I say "NOTHING!" I mean NOTHING will stop him from getting to know you, IF... that's what he truly wants!* But men, please be true to you and honest about why you are pursuing. If you stop approaching with wrong motives, then you will stop creating unnecessary situations. Especially when you know she is not "your wife." If you do start or continue to have a woman in your life knowing she is not "the one," you will end up with women fighting over you and eventually you end up sitting back taking advantage of the situation, because you figured out a way you could have both women. Now your nerves are wrecked! You started to look for peace and found it with someone else, because the "cat fight" is on and never ends with those two! Then one or both became pregnant and you decided to marry the new lady, knowing that you had

> *Men, God holds you accountable for the authority he has given you. Your wife should never feel uncertain about who she is to you. Remember, you are to love her like Christ loves the Church. The church is Christ's first priority!*
> *(Ephesians 5:25-29)*

to deal with both of them for the rest of your life. How crazy is that! This is what you will get men, if you don't **take charge of YOU...NOW!** Get focused on the will of God for your life, and don't approach a woman until you are ready to "date to marry."

In conclusion: Men of God, I challenge you to "reign in truth only, and make sure you are the Bishop of your life and your house" (I Timothy 3:1-2, Titus 1:7 KJV). Your responsibility is to establish and have dominion over your home, being sure to reign with truth and in love (I Corinthians 13 KJV). Keep in mind you should be doing this before you find her. Be sure not to give a woman your strength nor thy ways to that which will destroy kings. "Her husband is known in the gates when he sitteth among the elders in the land." He's highly esteemed and has good character. He operates with wisdom and he is not to drink wine, lest he forgets the law and perverts the judgment of any of the afflicted (Proverbs 31:1-9 & 23 KJV). This means don't give your position of power away by allowing your wife to do what you were created to do; get prepared to lead and provide for your family. Learn to do this with your "**finessed authority**" as I call it. It's so sexy when you can give instructions without offending or intimidating." Yeah...some women are "hardheaded...lol." She may buck!...and you might get the stare, but love on her anyway. Lean over and kiss her or take her hand and kiss it while looking at her saying "no, or not now my baby."

YES...EXPECTATIONS ARE NECESSARY!

Being equally yoked is as vital—"as breath is to life! Confess this and put it in your prayers – "I will not be unequally yoked together with an unbeliever; for what fellowship hath righteousness with unrighteousness? And what communion hath light with darkness?" (II Corinthians 6:14 KJV) **Yes, it's that deep; you are seeking to be joined in marriage... This is forever.**" Let us take a closer look into marriage. Are you looking? This is the union that God created. **He set the order** in which it should operate, so that His covenant would be fulfilled in the earth, from the ant family (tiniest with wisdom) to the human being family (intricate with His understanding). Marriage is not to be entered into lightly. Lightly, meaning without purpose.

> *The most effective way to reproduce is making sure that your actions and your words look alike.*
> **Staceylove**

Be clear on why you are entering into marriage. These *unions* produce families that reproduce itself again and again and so on. What would you like to see now and for generations to come in your family? It is up to you. **It starts with parents that have the same beliefs** (*each of you believe in Jesus, understand what marriage is the same way, think about raising the children the same way, become an entrepreneur, finishing school and getting a college degree, etc.*) I've heard stories about people dating then getting married who believe and serve God differently. In this type of commitment somebody will compromise their beliefs. Usually it's the woman because her husband is the head of the household (this is the order that God has set and it will not change). If she doesn't submit to the head of the household, she is out of order and there will be serious conflicts. Ladies, this means you should really pay attention to him, ask questions and most importantly - **listen to what** he is saying about what he will and won't do. If you think he will change because he loves you, **he will not.** Remember, it's not the love that he has for you; it's the love that God has for him that he must comprehend first. Then change will come for him. **Ladies hear this; (I'm putting it in a nutshell)**-when you agree to marry him…this is what he hears you saying and thinks that you understand…"I will forfeit what I believe for what you believe (if you don't believe the same), and I accept and agree to help (you're the help meet) you with all and everything that comes with you." The serious conflict is going to come when <u>you</u> finally realize that you are unequally yoked. Your husband is trying to lead the house hold from what he believes; you are taking a stand on what you believe; frustration has set in. Now you want out. What household can stand divided against itself? (*Mark 3:25 KJV*) People don't put your selves through this! Accept the order God has set for marriage ("family protocol"- Chapter 7) and get prepared to **operate from that stand point, once you get engaged and continue to date into marriage**. Another way to explain this is "being in sync and/or having harmony." (I Peter 3;1-9 KJV) Also in Genesis 2:24(KJV), God says… "and they shall be one flesh." And how else can two have harmony unless you believe the same?' This is why being equally yoked is **very, very important!**

It's ok that our approaches to Resolve Issues are Different!

> *Being equally yoked will also allow you to resolve issues better. This is a very important part of the process, because by the time it's time to resolve an issue or two you will be dating…saying I really like him/her "but sometimes he/she gets on my nerves!*

Ok, follow me now…when you first meet someone you're all nice, he or she's all nice. Both of you are all smiles and giggles. After about the fourth or fifth month, you are on your third or fourth date and something is said, discussed or a decision has to be made and you don't agree with the resolution given by the other person. You state your point or describe the way you would do it. In the midst of it all you went along with what the other person said, but you were harping (said or not) on the fact that it wasn't resolved your way! This is when it starts to get "real;" the relationship starts to open up! You start to see another side of each other. Typically, when people start to see something different than the "smiles and the giggles" they start to think "something is wrong." Not so, or is it? Most of the time, in this part of getting to know each other is where feeling "offended" starts. Mainly because every person thinks their resolution is the better way. This is where you should <u>pay attention to yourself</u>, to see if you really can communicate. Or shall I ask, are you willing to communicate? Resolving issues requires communication from both parties. Offense happens when a person wants to be heard, but they aren't because the other person is talking over them or when they finish listening and haven't <u>heard </u>a thing, so they go right back into explaining why their way is better. You must listen, so you can <u>understand</u> what is being said. Ask the necessary question(s) to be sure you are not assuming that you understand what you heard. Also be willing to answer the questions. Accept what you heard, and then make a decision on what is being discussed <u>at that time</u>. I encourage you to hear…because you want to be heard. (James 1:19-22 KJV) It's really ok to know how to share the responsibility of making decisions. *So, I present the Question!*

Are you accepting the person for who they are? Or are you trying to change them to be like you? Accepting them for whom and what they are is very important! If you accept, then you get to really know them. If you criticize them because they are not doing or saying it the way that you would, is trying to change them. We all act like this in the beginning, simply because we have not recognized that we are getting upset because the answer or the

> *Accepting them, is so that you can make an informed decision, about whether or not this person will be able to help cultivate your life for the purpose God has called you to. Note: be sure to pay close attention to this, because your bottom lines should be the same.*

way a person does something is different than the way you would answer or do it. **"Give** *what you want!"* **Accept because you want to be accepted.** *The good news is, if you don't try to change them, you will really get to see who they are.*

If you constantly criticize or try to get them to see or do things your way, that will make them insecure, now they are trying to please you by doing what you like. They are not being true to who they are…(Eventually resentment will set in). You don't want a person who is not true to themselves because then they can't be true to you.

Note: If you find that resolving issues continues to be a problem, heed the warning! **Marriage is not a cure all, it's a magnifier!**

You should expect to recognize the four types of love in your potential spouse.

The traits of the **Eros type of love are** enthusiasm, interest and excitement! This will spark "the play" in your relationship. I like to call this type of love "The Fire!" This will most likely be the first one many will recognize and certainly the one you will have to continuously tame!! This type of love is not to be degraded or ignored. Acknowledge it, but don't act on it yet!...wait until you say I do. Now I know this seems a little cut and dry...but you have to begin to think like this so that you can make it through the process. Then you will be able to act on all of those beautiful "play moments that was thought about and that you came really...close to acting on,..lol! **The Phileo type** of love represents friendship. This involves learning about each other's character, personality, temperament, how they respond in and to situations, and circumstances. It's important that you **like** who they are in all situations. When I say in all situations I mean over all, the best 4 ½ out of 5 and just make sure that, that half is still something you can live with. *Compromise is good, but not when it crosses over to challenging you to change who you are, what you believe to be true or the right thing to do. This will only set up resentment and lead to hatred if you are not truthful in all situations and under any circumstance.* **The Storge type of love** is where loyalty exists. This is the stage where you "know that you know," and can say "I can trust him/her." This is the place of certainty! Ladies, normally when a man reaches this stage, he is most likely to pursue and eventual propose because he has no doubt that "you've got his back." *And despite what the world says about losing weight, wearing long hair, lifting and tucking this and that to get a man, if he knows he can trust you and you do what the word of God says, you'll get there much faster!* Men, I urge you to let the "superficial part" of you go, so the recognition of your wife can be clearer. Storge and Phileo types of love will develop through conversation and interaction. This is also where the condition of the heart (sensitivities, insecurities, fears, beliefs, etc.) will be revealed. The word of God says "......for out of the abundance of the heart his mouth speaks." (Luke 6:45 KJV). **You must listen** and not take the words that you hear for granted. This is one of the most important scriptures pertaining to life, because what a person says (over and over again) comes from what he believes.

<u>What you believe has everything to do with how you operate. And the way you operate will determine the outcome of your life</u>. You must listen to <u>what you say</u> and know what you believe, as well as listening to others. **Note:** *Most of the time what you hear is not for you to correct, it's so you can make an informed decision!* **The Agape type of love** should be sited early in the friendship stages, but you will definitely see some of these traits as you start to develop the foundation for marriage; fidelity (dependable, trustworthy), acts of righteousness (honesty, morals) and humility. I want to encourage you to have expectations because when you do, it will help you not to just "go with the flow" when you meet someone. Let me explain. My mentality was everyone deserves the benefit of the doubt, along with listening to my girlfriends, "girl talk to him and just see what happens or "go get the free dinner." I'm here to tell you, everyone you meet doesn't deserve the benefit of talking to you further than the basic conversation,

> Friendships can be sustained by mutual interest, but commitment requires mutual interest and mutual beliefs.
>
> *Staceylove*

especially when you're in doubt! <u>Don't ignore the doubt you feel. Doubt is certain to mean something!</u> The "just see what happens part"…not if you're totally different and you know it. The "free dinner," how many of you know nothing truly is free…but salvation!

In conclusion: One might ask "how long am I to date a person?" It shouldn't take more than a year for him to know or her to accept. I believe men know almost immediately! Some women know almost immediately too, but definitely after a couple of seasons (six months) of dating. If you both operate in truth with yourself and each other while dating, you both will know in a reasonable time frame. Don't waste your time if you know the person is not the one! Don't be afraid that you are going to miss out; you won't! A girlfriend of mine and I always have said, you will find out the truth about the person right around the 90 day mark. The first 30 days you will see the "representative." It's just like everything else in life, in the beginning it's all new and shiny, smelling good and it's working well! In the span of the 60 days, you will know if you like the person or not and if you can deal with and/or adjust to all that you've learned after spending some quality time with them. If you haven't spent time with them, how can you make a determination as to who they are? Also, at this point you've begun to relax a little and be yourself and so have they. This is when you start to learn more about each other's lives, their families, the issues they have, and the issues other people have with them. Now you're in the 90 day home stretch (as I call it). There's something about the 90 day stretch. This is when a person starts to really get relaxed and then they just lay...on...down EVERYTHING! All the truths, the lies, it all will begin to unfold. The skeletons will start falling out of the closet, along with

Nutshell:

*The will of God is the word of God. In order to be in His will, you have to know what His word says. Ask Him for understanding.

*Gods' purpose for your life relates to how He uses you to help fulfill His covenant in the earth.

the live bodies that are hid up in there too!...lol. Now it's decision time. Compromise? Yes, in a relationship there is compromise, but not if it won't add to you. ***Remember, - <u>you are not</u> in a relationship in the first ninety days.*** And if you see the person needs to grow up spiritually, mental, financially, in decision making, giving, believing, etc. Don't feel that you have to grow through this with them <u>when you know</u> it will stop you from being in the will of God for your life. **Timing is everything**. Wait a while longer, apart. Remember, there is an order to everything. Make sure you are operating in order. You will know when it's your time to "date into marriage," but until then, work on developing in the purpose God has for your life!

PREPARING FOR MARRIAGE

TRANSITIONING FROM THE

SINGLE LIFESTYLE

TO THE

MARRIED LIFESTYLE

...are you ready?

"For the engaged Couple preparing for Marriage

Marriage is not based on what two individuals decide it will be. Marriage is a covenant created by God. He mandated the structure and purpose for it, and it won't ever change. The structure: man and woman marry and then cultivate their love and their lives. The purpose for marriage is for the couple to be fruitful and multiply, helping God fulfill His covenant in the earth (Genesis 1:28 & 35:11 KJV). **Fruitful** is to reproduce by having children, then they **multiply** by having children, creating generations. You should be knowledgeable about who she is, he is, and what they believe and who their parents are and what they believe. You will be continuing that bloodline and/or changing it to line up to God's word. In order to bring this about, both of you have to be equally yoked, be on the same page and in the same book (the word of God), walking and talking it out. The children you create <u>will do</u> what they see and <u>consider</u> what you say (Matthew 7:17-20 KJV). Marriage is a *lifestyle,* just as being single is a *lifestyle.* They run parallel to each other and they never intersect (as in mindset). Once you decide that it's time to leave the single lifestyle then you should start studying the married lifestyle (lifestyle = mindset). This doesn't mean that you can't have single friends. You just are not at liberty to do what they do anymore without your spouse (events, church, vacations, etc).

The Married Lifestyle (mindset) - "God's math is spiritual," when he added man and woman together he said "and they became one flesh" (Genesis 2:24 KJV). When you become one you are to focus on developing the mindset "we are one." I have spoken with many married men and women, after listening to their issues; so many times I have asked the question, "Why are you living single in your marriage?" Most times that was the underlying issue. They went back to their single mindset, or they never left it. Both of you have to be ready to convert your lifestyles, understand why you are getting married and the most important thing is to tell each other the whole truth about everything before you marry.

CHAPTER 6

PREPARING FOR THE MARRIAGE

(Especially for Men)

I Corinthians 13 KJV

A man that findeth a wife findeth a good thing and obtains favor from the Lord (Proverbs18:22 KJV). Men, what do you do after you have found her and she has accepted your request? You both are thinking about where you are going to live, the finances, the order that it all goes in. Are you really thinking about it the way God said to? Or did he say? Yes, he did. In Deuteronomy Chapters 20 and 24(KJV), it talks about taking responsibility for the pledge, a vow taken. Deuteronomy 24:5(KJV) says when a man has taken a new wife, he shall not go out to war, and neither shall he be charged with any business, but he shall be <u>free at home for one year</u>, and shall <u>cheer up</u> his wife which he hath taken (seized from life as she knew it). Hmmm…was my first thought when I read this, and then I began to study it. Then I asked God how we can relate this to us now? First, you should know that establishing a foundation for the family is one of God's highest priorities. Marriage is official God business! This is how He has chosen to replenish the earth. Marriage is His major pillar for fulfilling His will in the earth. He wants families to be strong and courageous; so that His will (legacy) and the family inheritance will be passed down from generation to generation. How do we relate and apply this scripture now?

- **The man should take a year off from the war**: not go into the service until after the first year of marriage.
- **And do no business**: not to start a business, or anything else, because you just <u>took this pledge</u>.

To make another pledge now would take your focus away from <u>establishing your household.</u> This pledge needs all of your time, prayers and undivided attention. Allow the Holy Spirit to give you guidance. Your loyalty to this pledge/covenant in the first year will greatly determine the success of your marriage for many years to come. In the first year of establishing your household, learn to <u>show</u> her your commitment. Continue counseling. <u>Acknowledge the pledge,</u> and remind yourself to be and stay loyal to it. <u>Speak about your pledge</u> often, to yourself and in conversation with your friends and family. When you get married, you are making the choice to serve God first, and to do things according to the covenant of marriage.

The bible says that a man is to love his wife as Christ loves the church (Ephesians 5:17-33 KJV, this is the covenant). The church is God's first priority. So should your wife be to you. Why does she need to be cheered up? Before marrying, her focus was on her safe keeping/security, friendships and social groups, etc., things that she must adjust, reduce or put to the side. This will be challenging for her in the beginning, because those relationships defined her life. In the adjustment of becoming a married woman, you are now her second largest priority (God being her first), and she will need your undivided attention, (the more independent she is the more attention she may require). You are her first line of defense now; you are her

> Men, it doesn't matter about your age, if you have a 9-5 or a conglomerate of businesses, Gods plan for taking a wife stays the same!
>
> -Take off one year to establish your household and cheer up your new wife.
> -Make strategic plans for your household.

covering. You are the provider for the family and she needs to know this, feel this and have absolutely no questions about this. These are the things you will be helping her adjust to in this first year. Can she safely trust you? Trust begins with you. Show your trust and be willing to allow her to be trusted. Whenever she has an issue make sure you are there to listen and/ or to help resolve, if needed. Remember guys, not every issue she has needs your opinion or a solution; sometimes she just needs you to listen to her (not talking about life changing issues). Learn her. Get to know when she is venting and when she needs your help solving an issue. Just in case you can't tell the difference.....ask her. After you have listened attentively, then you look at her and say "baby?, am I just listening, or would you like my opinion? Men, let me also say this, never mind that stuff about "men are impatient and women talk too much." Telling her to talk to her girlfriend about that…or you don't have time to listen…...**No!! Don't you tell her that**, or make her feel like she can't come to you with EVERYTHING. You are supposed to know everything and the same with you, she is to know EVERYTHING. Go to her and tell her everything, not someone else. If you are in order, it will be easier for her to be with you and talk with you. Your intent has to be **unmistakably clear!** There should be

> **Yes… Ladies!** You must listen and ask the same question to him, "are you just listening or does he want your opinion?

no privacy in your relationship…you are one. If you are harboring your phone, and he or she can't answer it or pick it up without you "stroking out," you are hiding something. If your friends are not her friends or her friends are not your friends, you are hiding something. If you are hiding anything other than a birthday gift, your intentions are wrong!! GET IN ORDER…QUICK!! Just like God has an order for the church (the laws and statutes for order and the commands for instruction), He expects the man to establish his house by and with the same order. This takes time to establish (one year, minimum). To be clearer, men stay **focused** on this. **Study** the word of God on these things. **Do** what the word of God says only and continue in it:

1st -_**Tell**_ the truth – it may feel like it will hurt you…but it will set you free and you will begin to heal.

2nd -You must _**know**_ the true definition of Love according to the word of God. (Chapter one)

3rd -You must _**pray**_ according to the word of God. If the scripture says renew your mind, He means renew your mind about what the word of God says to do about everything. Trust it and do it. You must do your part. Heal from the fear of telling the truth.

4th - **Tithe**. Tithing is one of the physical acts of _**trusting in**_ the word of God. This is paramount! Make sure you study it out and do it.

5th – Therefore, all things whatsoever ye would that men should do to you, do ye even so to them: for this is the law and the prophets. (Matthew 7:12 KJV) "Do unto others as you would have them do unto you." I like to say this in the simplest form, **give what you want!**

59

Imagine. If we could just remember these five very important things and apply them to all situations first, the results of our relationships and our lives in general, will be so much better!

Now that you have lined up spiritually, there are some things you must do in the physical.

- You and your wife must sit down pray and write the "Family Creed" for your household (what is your vision for the family?). Find scriptures to print and display in the house.
- Establish your household rules and goals, such as curfews or set times for breakfast, dinner and family meetings, etc.)
- Household Family times: birthdays, vacations, date nights, personal time, etc.
- Entire Family: celebrations and vacations

These are the things that will set the foundation for your family. God gave man a role and the woman a role for the relationship. Man is the headship (leader) and the woman is the help meet. Men, being the headship/leader have one main purpose: "to serve the needs of another and to make sure your decisions will benefit the well-being of everyone involved." God intended for your role to be in favor of your household, not for "control" or instilling fear for dependency. When God talks about a man and a woman being subject to each other, He meant just that. Not because you are the "head of the house and "what I say goes and what your wife says is null and void." If you use your authority this way, God looks at it as being out of order. It means your intentions are not pure, and you are using your authority to manipulate the situation to benefit only you, whether it's for you to make room to cheat, lie, or steal. The characteristics of your headship should be like the fruit of the spirit: love, joy, peace, longsuffering, gentleness, goodness, and faith, and meekness, temperance: against such there is no law. (Galatians 5:22-26 KJV)

Please do not establish your household like "mama-nem," if "mama-nem" wasn't doing it the way God said to do it...

Women, help meet means to be the support system for your husband. Also there are some other things you are held responsible for…being the wife:

- **To reverence your husband**. This is a command. Meaning, you must respect him. Let me explain it in another way for better clarity. Let's say you are in a public place and you see a priest walk in, and immediately you feel a sense of respect for him because of the honor of the position that he represents. This is the same type of reverence you are to give to your husband, because of the position of honor he holds. You must do this wifey! (I'm smiling…) Keep in mind ladies, respect has parts to it. The first one is **listening to him attentively.** Meaning you are hearing what he is saying and being able to repeat back what he said to you, then bringing your-self into **agreement** with him! Most times we agree but then we want to tell him "how we would do it." No ladies, doing it the way he said is the other part of respecting him. This is where you trust that God has instructed him and that he will yield to what the Lord has told him. Instead of saying anything to him about the way you would do it, encourage him to go to the word of God for wisdom. Now you pray, "Lord I thank you for giving my husband wisdom and guidance, and that he will ask in faith. You said in your word Lord, that as he commits his work unto you, his thoughts shall be established. Now you sit back trust God and your husband. (Philippians 4:6, Ephesians 5: 33 KJV, James 1:5 KJV, Proverbs 16:3 KJV)

- To **submit yourself** to your husband. Submission is for your protection ladies. That's why God mandated him to be the head of the house. You will be vulnerable, but that's why you must trust in the word of God that he is living by. <u>I urge you to know whose word he is living by before you take these vows.</u> (Ephesians 5: 21-24 KJV)

- Another part of reverencing is **reserving your affections** for your husband and your children, in that order. (Titus 2: 3-5 KJV) Your verbal affection should be parallel to your non-verbal (body language) affection.

Another very important thing you both must understand is the principle of **leaving and cleaving.** (Genesis 2:24 KJV) Well, its "kind of" self explanatory, but I feel a need to say this because of the ratio of couples that I have met that don't have a clue about what this means. In Gods eyes, when a man and woman take this vow they are saying they understand that He sees you as <u>one</u>, not just together as one "**really as one.**" (Ephesians 5:29-33 KJV)

There's no more mine and yours. Everything you own she owns, and everything she owns you own. For clarity, **everything…**the children, houses, cars, land, jewelry, business, friends, and cell phones etc. Another very important part to focus on while establishing your households is how you spend your time. This chart shows the percentage of the time that should be spent in each area. Children's activities fall in the household family category (7%). This is important to know because often the children and their activities trade places with the husband/wife category (40%). The children are very important, but always remember you are raising children to become responsible adults. Your ability to hold these percentages intact is what will enable your children to leave and have the same percentages in their household. The career category (5%) is second to your household family. The income is important but when your focus stays on the God/Prayer/ Tithing category (45%) you won't have a problem in this area. The family and friends category (3%) is still probably 2% percent too much, but please be sure you don't allow this category to override any of the others. If you do, it will be like driving a wedge through your family's foundation and most families don't survive that. A family may survive this but why go through this when all you have to do is set your house in order and stand by it. The numbers may be a little extreme, but you need to understand the importance of this.

45%God/Prayer/Tithe
40%Husband/Wife
7%Household/Family
5% Career
3% Family & Friends

Men, are you still with me? I know this seems complex, but so is anything that is worth having. Once you make the commitment to operate Gods way, all of this will become first nature to you. Don't make it hard; just do it! This is the way to get all God has for you and your family. **Another important area for you to pay close attention to while engaged and getting prepared to establish your home is <u>not to have sex before</u>**

you get married. Men hold your selves accountable to this. Reserve your body for your wife. Women are known for being able to abstain from intimacy longer than men. **But men, this has to change** and it starts with you prioritizing, which means doing things decent and in sequential order. You are given and charged with these responsibilities by God because you are the headship of your household, even if you are single right now. **Don't allow yourself to be setup** and put in a situation that will lead you out of righteousness and/or order. Women can be manipulative, conscious of it or not. However, don't worry about her; focus on making sure that you are aware and **in control** of yourself. I need to be graphic here for the ones that need it. If you are looking at porn and/or while at the mall your eyes are following every butt you see…STOP IT! Control yourself. "They" say ain't nothing wrong with looking. **Yes, it is** when you start drooling. "They" say men are visual first, and now you believe it and use it as an excuse in choosing a mate. Also choosing a woman based on what "your boys" will say? And you wonder why you continually end up with a "fine woman" that disrespects, and degrades you and the call on your life. She never encourages or compliments you. She uses you, oh - but that's ok because she's the "eye candy," not for you but mainly for "your boys." If the truth be told, you really don't like her because she can't hold a decent conversation, and she goes to church but she's stuck on doing what she wants to do and not willing to do what God says to do. Stop listening to what "they" say (the World and your boys) and go with what you know is right (your gut feeling). When you do meet a woman, remember, you must stop and think about what to say, and you must gauge how you are feeling in order to determine if you are going to proceed. You have to be aware of the mindset you're in at that time. Is it your shallow-superficial self? Is it your horny self? Or is it your sensible, ready to be committed self? If you meet a woman and you feel like you can "take her or leave her," do both of you a favor and leave her! As I always say, you will know when you meet "her." You won't be able to quite explain it in the beginning. You won't know why "she" has taken over and you're driven to be with "her", and it's not sexual! That feeling is significant. You will not want to be without her, and in every way "she just makes sense!" You should get to know each other emotionally first, how you both feel about church, career/work, life, family, etc. and understand why you feel that way. I use the word emotions because when you meet someone your emotions are going wild and you're trying not to react to them, but don't know what to do first. <u>To gain control of your emotions is to understand they are directly in line with your senses; see, smell, hear and touch.</u> Seeing and smelling is connected with your imagination. You must speak the word of God (I cast down imaginations, and every high thing that exalted itself against the knowledge of God so you can turn on your hearing emotion, to gain control over the first two emotions. (2 Cor. 10:5 KJV) Last but often put first is your touching emotion. You must pay close attention to this emotion, because it is the maximum level of emotions (intimacy-sex). It's like driving a five speed car. You just met the person—1st gear, shift—getting to know them, shift—now you know if she is the right one, shift—you ask for her hand in marriage—she accepts, you marry, now you can shift in to 5th gear and drive that baby! But if you start having sex before you marry, you gone mess the car up! If you know about driving a five speed, you know if you strip any of the gears you will never be able to drive the car with its full potential, or if at all.

In conclusion, marriage is a life style! Men you are the first one God gave the original commandment to, so you are held accountable to keep it. It starts with you, and the woman was made to be in sync with that which God commanded you. You are choosing to take a wife, now it is your responsibility to <u>provide and care for her</u>. Make no excuses; make a ***righteous*** way to take care of her. Just for more clarity, you pay the mortgage/rent. You make sure the lights are on in the house and food is on the table, for starters. This is parallel to how Christ loves the church. If you get your thinking in line with the word of God and <u>begin to do</u> it, then the families you produce will reproduce what you have set in order! The biggest trick of the devil is telling you that nobody can tell you what it is to be a man *but a man*. I urge you not to look at the messenger, just hear the message. I keep hearing people say, "I'm a realist; I'm just keeping it real." So I pose the Question?...what is your reality? Let your reality line up with the word of God, and speak that only. No, that is not the popular thing to do, but do you want to keep receiving the popular thing, divorce, lack, fear, pre-mature death? I hope not. Or do you want to receive ALL the promises of God? I hope you do, because you can! But it will require you to know, speak and do the word of God.

CHAPTER 7

LOVE & MONEY?

I Corinthians 13 (KJV)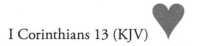

Yes!....Love and money can go together! It's a touchy subject even for the people who are in love. The only way to deal with "love and money" is to have total honesty with one self. If you are good with money...great! If you're not, admit it, so you can move forward! It's not ok that you're not good with the money, but the problem comes in when you can't admit it to yourself, and if you are not willing to change for the good of <u>your</u> own well-being, ok. But you are...let's say that this has not been a main focus, but you do pay your bills and you have been able to save a little. If your potential spouse is someone who pays their bills on time, good with multiplying his or her money, or is more disciplined, then that is the better person to take responsibility of the household finances until you are better. God expects both of you to be good stewards over ALL of the money, not just the bill money.

Talking about money is like talking about sex...SCARY!!! If we are going to change the heritage of our families, we must prepare to and change the money issues. The word of God says that a good man leaves an inheritance to his children's children and the wealth of the sinner is laid up for the just. (Proverbs 13:22 KJV) In order for us to get the money thing right, we must understand what the word says about money; how to get it, what to do with it and why. First, we know we must work. I don't believe God meant for you to just work any old job just to have some money to pay your bills. I believe that work should be tied to your purpose. Purpose is the reason God created you. Your purpose can be identified as that thing that you do effortlessly

> **FYI...shhh...**keep quiet about your purpose and plans! Most of your family and friends won't be able to "see" what you have been shown...in the beginning.

and love it! It brings' you joy and peace when you are doing it. Keep working where you are working, identify your purpose. Get prepared, and then start your transition so that you can begin to work in your purpose. In Matthew 25 (KJV), when Jesus was ministering to the people He told them two parables. The first one is about being prepared (be wise = preparation or be foolish = unprepared). Now, let me say…being prepared doesn't mean it will be easy all the time. It means that you are better equipped to handle situations that will occur. Getting prepared; going to school or getting educated will help you to hone in/groom yourself for your purpose. He also talked about the talents = gift = purpose….and He gave them to <u>every man</u> according to his <u>several ability</u>. Remember, your purpose is tied to your gifts. We are supposed to multiply the gift(s) and bring them back with usury = interest. The Lord talks about how He is proud that you managed the gift(s) well and now you can be in charge of more. Now you can enter into the joy (delight) of the Lord. This is why it is important for us to understand tithing, offerings, and alms; yes it is all linked to your purpose. **Tithes** are the tenth of <u>all your earnings.</u> Your earning is what you worked for. This is not yours to decide what to do with. The first tenth belongs to God (this is a law). When you tithe that says to God, I trust your word. (Leviticus 27:30-34 KJV, Malachi 3 KJV). How and when do you start to apply biblical knowledge to your life? Immediately! Sit down and figure out what you need to pay according to your gross earnings. Go to your church website, and pay your tithes. If necessary, get a money order and go to the church immediately and drop your tithe in the tithe and offering box. Sometimes you have to go to "the extreme" to get committed! If you receive a check, it's 10% of your gross income (before taxes), not the amount of the check. Self-employed people, or individuals who make money every day it's important to take your tithes out every day, put them to the side or go to "the extreme." Once you see Gods word working in your life, you will never go back to not tithing. Did somebody say how long will that take?.... As soon you believe and do the word, or as soon as you do and believe the word you will see the difference. Make Gods word your final authority (Galatians 6:7). Proverbs 3:5-6(KJV), it says "Trust in the Lord with all thine heart; <u>and lean not unto thine own understanding.</u> <u>In all thy </u>ways acknowledge him and he shall direct thy paths. In Malachi 3:10(KJV), the Lord said "take care of my house—the church, and He will take care of yours. Prove me now, (test me) and see won't I pour you out a blessing (increase your business/bring you a promotion/new business, give you an idea), that you won't have room enough to receive it. Malachi 3:11(KJV) says, and he will rebuke (stop) the devourer (anything or person that tries to consume and/or destroy your ideas), for your sake, and he shall not destroy the fruit (increase) of your ground: nor shall your vine cast her fruit before the time in the field (what you planted/your ideas will not wither and die, it will bloom fully), saith the Lord of hosts. Malachi 3:12(KJV) says, and all nations shall call you blessed (your success will be seen), and you will be a delightsome land (you will be a joy, giving pleasure/distribution center) saith the Lord of host. I've been asked what I thought about taking your tithes and giving it to someone in need. The person said, it was good and it was what God wanted them to do. That would be an offering or alms (a sacrifice). Your tithes are not to be used for anything else, but to be given to your church (Gods' house, where the true word of God is coming forth) for the work that's being done there to further the Kingdom. **"Being nice" does not come before being obedient.** *Tithing is first, PERIOD.* My man of God always says "we don't come to church to be a Christian; that's just what Christian's do, go to church." The same with tithing, that's just what Christians do! **An offering is** anything you give <u>after</u> the tithe, your sacrifice. This is how we can get what we <u>want</u> and "keep yo money from being funny...lol." (II Corinthians 9). **Alms** are acts of righteousness and should be done in secret (Mathew 6:4 KJV). *This is my personal testimony* about getting the money thing right. I say the "money thing" because having "love" was way more important to me than "making money!" And it still is, but the Lord kept pulling my coattail about my perspective about the money. So...I was making money, paying my tithes and still didn't have enough to pay my bills. I will never forget, I was praying and asking the Holy Spirit what I was doing wrong? I'm paying my tithes. He spoke to me clearly, "what are you doing with your <u>need money</u>?" He did say He would supply our needs according to His riches in glory through Christ Jesus (Philippians 4:19 KJV). My mindset was "as long as I paid my tithes I'm good." I was so excited about paying my tithes, but I wasn't being a good steward (managing) over the "need money," not realizing that the need money is not the "want money." After I got that right, I went back to the Holy Spirit and said "ok now I want some things for me?" I had some money left over, but I have "Champagne Taste!" This is when I had to study about the offerings. In 2 Corinthians 9:6-15(KJV), Paul talks about sowing sparingly and sowing bountifully. It goes on talking about how we will have sufficiency in all things, and how your seed will be multiplied. (I encourage you to study the entire chapter) So…I kept hearing "to whom much is given much is required." (Luke 12:48 KJV) I heard it through a sermon; I heard it on the radio. I saw it in something I was reading. It was just ever present! So I had to ask "God, what are you trying to tell me?" And I kept hearing it…but it just didn't make sense to me. I know it sounds like I should understand what that means but it just wasn't making sense to me! I'm sure somebody is asking why? Well I knew that because I kept seeing and hearing it, that meant I needed to study it out for understanding. First, I thought this phrase had something to do with material possessions. Well, my possessions at that time…well lets' just say I didn't have a lot of material goods…the basic stuff, car, apartment and some clothes, etc. I knew He couldn't be talking about material things, because if He was it would have stated it somewhere in the word…the house, car etc. Then I asked again "what are you talking about Lord?" Divine revelation came when I heard the message again about the parable of the sower in Mark 4(KJV). We are all familiar-as in listening to it, but this time I heard it! I'll never forget, I was in the mist of studying, I had just gone back to read Mark 4:19(KJV) again, and just as divine revelation came…***I was sitting there appalled because I had just found out that "I wasn't good ground!!...like I had been proclaiming!"***…and here comes my daughter in the house ranting and-raving about something… and wanted me to stop, listen and come see! There it was…the cares of the world! I almost couldn't believe this was happening at that moment…a distraction! I had to make a decision. I was staring at her….she was talking loud and looking at me like…I need you now!...and I couldn't move!...I said "NO!" In my head I'm saying "I can't get up and move away from hearing the Holy Spirit…because I had to become good ground as soon as possible!!.., like NOW! I know you are saying, "How does this relate to "whom much is given, much is required?" It relates because "the much" that is given is the understanding = divine revelation of the word of God! In order for me to be "the good ground" I had to choose to accept this knowledge then bring forth fruit (which is tied to my purpose).... and that is the "<u>requirement!</u>" OMGoodness!!!!... I got it, I got it I understand!....... at that moment my head was spinning and I'm jumping up and down on the inside, and my daughter is still standing there looking at me like something has got to be wrong with her!....Yawl...I was kinda shocked too, that I wasn't moving (like I usually do) and the only word I could get out was NO!... That was a trip...I closed the books and went to bed!....

Now, picture your purpose as a tree.

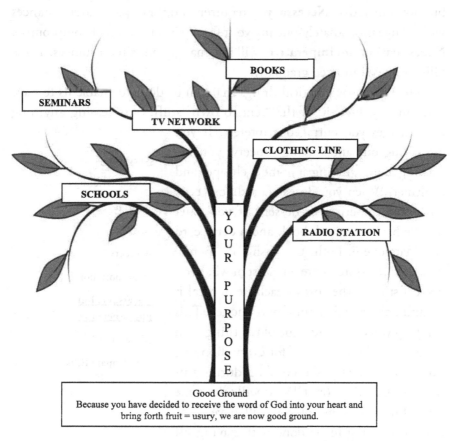

I am thanking God in advance that you are <u>willing</u> to put "your personal beliefs and opinions" down and <u>hear</u> the word of God. How do you hear? By speaking it...this cultivates the ground of your heart so that you can receive the word of God. Once your heart is filled with the word of God then your mouth will speak it. (Luke 6:45 KJV) Now you will begin to see what you are saying. The word of God is not "common sense." You must choose to make it apart of your common sense then it will become the norm.

The practical way of mastering the money. There are two keys to the word of God "working" for you. 1. You must **believe** it will work for you, and then you must **work it**! Please lose the mind set "if it happens…..YAY!! And if it doesn't, I'll just deal with that. We are going to sit down and write down everything to be paid, prioritizing the order. Let's not complicate it or make any more excuses. Use two categories, necessary and necessary but not imperative. **Necessary**- a requirement; if not paid, circumstances will change immediately-putting your family in a position of compromise. **Necessary but not imperative**- will not change your circumstances. These bills can be eliminated gradually.

Here are some practical things that can be done to enable us to have extra money. Get rid of the "rent to own" stuff. Stop leasing anything that charges you outrageous interest. If you are eating out and buying grocery, you are wasting money. Eating at home is cheaper and healthier. When you do eat out choose two: an entrée, appetizer or dessert. If you can't handle having a check book and a debit card eliminate one or both. Use cash only. Before you go to the store, write out a list of what you need. Estimate the cost of each item, total it up and only take that amount of money. This can help you eliminate some of the things you could do without. Do this for every shopping experience. Don't give up or faint during this process. (Galatians 6:9 KJV) It will take some time. Like me, some of you will have some days of wanting to be done with paying off people and bills! Just stick to speaking the word of God. Do the word the word of God. Now see the word of God. Final note for the believer…. God is not a respecter of persons. His word says, be truthful…be truthful. His word says, believe that I AM. Believe that He Is. His word says, my ways are not your ways. Stop thinking that

<u>Necessary</u>

-Tithes/Offerings

-Mortgage/Rent

-Utilities

-Grocery

-Transportation

<u>Necessary, but not imperative</u>

-Credit Cards

-Old Unpaid Bills

He will do it the way you would and when you would. He also said He's watching over His word to perform it, you must speak it! Trust Him and you will see His word manifest. Philippians 4:6-9(KJV), James 1:3-4(KJV), Proverbs 13:22(KJV), Galatians 6:7(KJV), Psalms 138:8(KJV), James 1:25 (KJV). Romans 2:11(KJV) Jeremiah 1:12 (KJV) Isaiah 55:8 (KJV) Proverbs 8:32 (KJV)

Final conclusion: OMGoodness! I am soooo excited about the divine revelations I've gotten! Remember…living for God is one way, meaning He has a system. The system is, knowing how He operates, and then operating in the order He has set for everything. First, you must **Believe** – (this is a law) have faith in the word of God. (Ephesians 2:8, Mark 11:22, Mark 9:23 KJV) Next, you must be **Honest and Truthful** – this is the only way to serve God. (John 4:24, Ephesians 4 KJV) Then you must **Love** – (this is the new command) (John 13.34, I Corinthians 13, Galatians 5:22-26 KJV). Lastly we must remember that **Seedtime and Harvest will always exist** – this is a law (Genesis 8:22 KJV), whatever you plant, that's what you will harvest. There are three areas you can plant in, the heart ground… by what you speak (reap in the body, soul & and spirit). (Proverbs 12:14 KJV) The church ground…paying your tithes (1st 10% of all your income) and sowing your offerings (reap in spirit that manifest in the tangible form in the earth, by way of giving money). (Malachi 3:10-12 KJV) And the ground….Reap tangibly, this will produce food for the body and/or money to sow and live on. I must tell you, once God gives you divine revelation about His word, He holds you accountable. (Luke 12:48 KJV).

I wrote this book because of the passion I have for Love, Marriage and Relationships. I want to see Marriages work! And I don't mean "work it out!" I just believe that if we began to live in truth and understand the order that God set for marriage before we get married, we will see until death do us part marriages from generation to generation. I've learned so much while writing this book. I thought I knew a lot about the Lord, **now I really do.** The Holy Spirit said to me one night during the close of writing, "why limit yourself?... living by the boundaries man has set for you, because of their fears. I have no limits, only endless possibilities if you only believe." I have gotten away from my fears and I just believe! I believe what the word of God says, **period.** And if what you say, the media says, my mama said, isn't found in the word of God, I'm NOT going by it, bottom line!! I truly believe the word of God is that simple **–in a Nutshell.** Get understanding and do what the word of God says and you get what He said. I'm FREE! (Jumping up, clicking my heels together – FREE!!) I have truly enjoyed being obedient to the Spirit of Christ. I've grown through this process and I know that you will too! (Hebrews 4:2-3 KJV, 1 Timothy 4:15-16 KJV)

TRUE

    LOVE HAS NO FEAR

TRUE

    LOVE STANDS...COURAGEOUS

TRUE

    LOVE IS RADIANT

TRUE

    LOVE SPEAKS LOUD WITHOUT MAKING A SOUND

Staceylove

I Corinthians 13 (KJV)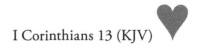

Printed in the United States
By Bookmasters